Things
TO DO
WITH
Mom

WRITTEN BY ALISON MALONEY
ILLUSTRATED BY KAREN DONNELLY
EDITED BY SALLY PILKINGTON
DESIGNED BY ZOE QUAYLE

Things TO DO WITH Mom

SCHOLASTIC INC.

New York   Toronto   London   Auckland   Sydney
Mexico City   New Delhi   Hong Kong   Buenos Aires

No part of this publication may be reproduced, stored in a retrieval system, or transmitted in any form or by any means, electronic, mechanical, photocopying, recording, or otherwise, without written permission of the publisher. For information regarding permission, write to Michael O'Mara Books Limited, 9 Lion Yard, Tremadoc Road, London SW4 7NQ, United Kingdom.

Library of Congress Cataloging-in-Publication Data
Maloney, Alison.
Things to do with mom / written by Alison Maloney ; illustrated by
Karen Donnelly ; edited by Sally Pilkington ; designed by Zoe Quayle.
p. cm.
ISBN-13: 978-0-545-13401-9
ISBN-10: 0-545-13401-3
1. Recreation—Juvenile literature. 2. Amusements—Juvenile literature.
3. Play—Juvenile literature. 4. Mother and child--Juvenile literature.
1. Pilkington, Sally. ll. Donnelly, Karen, ill. lll. Title.
GV182.9.M35 2008
790.1'91—dc22   2008039867

First published in Great Britain in 2008 by Michael O'Mara Books Limited,
9 Lion Yard, Tremadoc Road, London SW4 7NQ, United Kingdom.
www.mombooks.com

Text copyright © 2008 Michael O'Mara Books
Illustrations copyright © 2008 Karen Donnelly
Cover design by Angie Allison
Cover illustration by Paul Moran

12 11 10 9 8 7 6 5 4 3 2 1   9 10 11 12 13 14/0

Printed in the U.S.A.
First American edition, April 2009

Contents

Introduction

"Mom, I'm bored!"

It's a phrase that fills every busy mother with dread. It usually means that she'll end up spending an hour or two playing a tedious board game or will give in and let the children watch yet another DVD.

But it doesn't have to be like that. Put a little time aside to enjoy one another's company and do something fantastic together instead. .

This helpful book is packed with activities for both adults and children to enjoy. Some are practical, some are artistic, some are just plain indulgent — but they are all guaranteed to be lots of fun.

Whether you have ten minutes or a whole day, this book has a perfect activity for you. Simple instructions mean you can try arts and crafts, games, recipes, pampering ideas, magic tricks, and much, much more.

Look for these hand symbols throughout to ensure fingers get chocolatey and muddy, but not burned.

 This symbol indicates tasks that are best for moms to perform.

 This symbol is for tasks that kids will enjoy.

So go ahead — banish that boredom!

How Does Your Miniature Garden Grow?

Miniature gardens are extremely versatile. They can provide a handy windowsill kitchen garden, a tropical jungle for a toy T. rex to roam in, or an enchanted fairy kingdom. You can even re-create the Hanging Gardens of Babylon in miniature.

PREPARATION

The beauty of a miniature garden is that it can be created anywhere. You may have a window box or flower bed you could use, or you may prefer to use a pot or tray so that you can move your garden wherever you like.

Select your plants. For this you need to decide whether yours is an indoor or an outdoor garden, as this will affect the type of plants that you choose. It is a good idea to ask a staff member at your local garden center to help with your selection. He or she will be able to recommend interesting plants that are suited to your garden's soil and climate. Here are some ideas to get you started.

IDEAS FOR INDOOR PLANTS

- miniature boxwood
- scented miniature cyclamen
- miniature roses
- miniature African violets
- herbs (parsley, basil, rosemary)

IDEAS FOR OUTDOOR PLANTS

- honeysuckle
- ferns (ideal for shady spots)
- miniature weeping willow
- miniature jasmine
- miniature grass

PLANNING

Next you need to decide how you are going to arrange your garden. Draw a garden plan, taking into account the shape of your plot or container. When drawing your plan, you should add any features you want to include, such as benches, arches, or water features. You should also indicate where you are going to have any gravel paths or stepping stones.

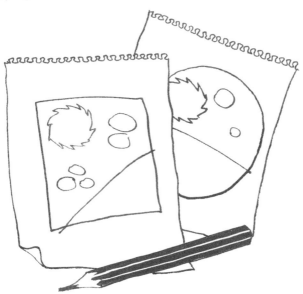

PLANTING

Once you have your plants and have designed your garden, it's time to begin planting.

Place a brick or a paving stone at the bottom of your container. Add some gravel or pebbles for drainage. Then spread your compost so it is about 4 inches deep.

Dig holes in the compost and then carefully remove the plants from their plastic pots. Place the plants in the holes and fill around them with earth, pressing down firmly on the soil. Once all the plants are in place, you can add your decorative features (see the suggestions below).

IDEAS FOR GARDEN FEATURES

- Decks: Use small pieces of wood, twigs, or Popsicle sticks.

- Patios: Use small stones and pebbles.

- Mountain ranges: Use larger stones.

- Paths: Colored gravel for fish tanks works well and can be bought from garden centers or pet stores.

- Furniture: You may have dollhouse furniture you could use, but be careful in outdoor gardens as it could be damaged by the weather.

- Water features: These can be relaxing places for the tiny inhabitants of your garden or a watering hole for a toy velociraptor. They can be made from a small mirror or a sunken dish filled with water. Float a leaf and a small flower on this, and it will look like a beautiful water lily.

• Marbles: You can buy these at most florists or craft stores. They make magical additions to the landscape.

UPKEEP

Your miniature garden will need regular watering. Make sure you keep the borders neat, and trim any plants that look like they are becoming unruly. New features like birdbaths or statues can be added whenever you feel like giving the garden a completely new look.

Delicious Chocolate Chip Muffins

These delicious treats are perfect to make for parties, picnics, or presents, or just because they are so yummy. Eat them warm, not long after they have come out of the oven, when the chocolate chips are still melted and gooey. Or, if you can manage to resist them, store in an airtight container for another day.

You will need:

- 4 tablespoons butter or margarine
- 3/4 cup milk • 2 eggs • 2 cups flour
- 1/2 teaspoon salt • 2 teaspoons baking powder
- 1/4 cup sugar • 1/2 cup chocolate chips
- 12-cup muffin pan • 12 muffin liners

Preheat the oven to 400°F.

Melt the butter (either in a microwave or in a bowl placed in hot water). Mix the butter, milk, and eggs in a large bowl.

Combine the flour, salt, baking powder, and sugar in a separate bowl. Make a well in the center of the dry ingredients with a wooden spoon, and pour the liquid

ingredients into it. Mix well. Add the chocolate chips and stir.

 Spoon the mixture into the muffin liners placed either in a muffin pan or on a baking tray. Fill each halfway. This mixture should fill a dozen liners.

Place the muffins in the oven. Bake for 20 minutes or until they have risen and are a golden color.

Leave the muffins to stand for a few minutes and then remove them from the pan and cool on a wire rack.

Enjoy!

Make Your Own Place Mat

Brighten up mealtimes with a personalized place mat of your own unique design. Make it a family collage or a work of art, an explosion of color or a stylish piece of interior design. Whatever you choose, it beats boring store-bought place mats any day. Why not make a set for the whole family? Here are two methods for creating a mat masterpiece.

THE ARTISTIC METHOD

You will need:

- paint, crayons, or felt-tip markers
- a sheet of paper (8 1/2 inches by 11 inches)
- a sheet of cardboard (8 1/2 inches by 11 inches)
- a glue stick • clear contact paper

Get creative. You are now a designer of exclusive place mats. Draw a picture, a pattern, or a series of shapes on your paper – you could even draw your favorite meal.

When the design is done, glue it to the sheet of cardboard and then cover both sides with clear contact paper, being careful to smooth it out (as instructed on the packaging) so no bubbles are trapped.

Set the table with your new designer place mats.

THE COLLAGE METHOD

You will need:

- collage materials (photos, magazine pictures, foil wrapping paper, stickers, stars, etc.)
- a glue stick
- a sheet of paper (8 1/2 inches by 11 inches)
- pens • a sheet of cardboard (8 1/2 inches by 11 inches)
- clear contact paper

Choose the pictures you want for the place mat. Family photos look much nicer if they are cut in irregular shapes, rather than square. Glue the pictures to the paper and decorate around them with your other collage materials. Personalize your mat further by writing your name in bold letters.

When the design is done, glue it to the sheet of cardboard and cover both sides with clear contact paper. Alternatively, take your place mat to a copy shop that can laminate it for you.

Make Your Own Luxurious Chocolate Truffles

Homemade truffles make wonderful gifts for friends and family. The bonus in making your own is that you know exactly what goes into them, and there are no artificial preservatives.

These decadent balls of chocolate are deceptively simple to make. Experiment with different extracts to create brand-new flavors.

You will need:

- 5 ounces good quality chocolate
- 3/4 cup heavy cream
- 2 tablespoons unsalted butter
- 1 tablespoon vanilla extract (optional)
- 1/2 tablespoon cocoa powder

Grate the chocolate using a grater.

In a pan, bring the cream and the butter to a boil and then remove from the heat. Stir in the grated chocolate, a little at a time, until it is all combined and you have a rich, dark chocolatey mix.

Add the vanilla extract and stir. Transfer the mixture to a bowl and leave it to cool and solidify.

Now for the fun part. Once the mixture is solid, use a teaspoon to scoop out blobs of mixture. Roll them between your palms to make little bite-size balls. The mixture will get sticky as your hands warm up, so dust your hands with cocoa powder from time to time. Place the balls on a baking tray.

Put some cocoa powder on a plate and roll each of the balls in it until they are evenly covered. Your yummy truffles are now ready.

Tip from Mom: Put your truffles in plastic eggs for a delightful Easter gift.

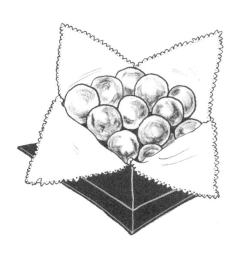

Mind Reading with Mom

This trick requires two people to be "in the know." Mom will be the mind reader, and the other person will be her assistant.

The assistant stands in front of the audience, and Mind-reading Mom leaves the room. The assistant asks the members of the audience to choose an object in the room. He or she then tells the audience that Mind-reading Mom will return to the room and be able to "read" which item has been chosen. Sure enough, she does.

HOW TO DO IT

In private, before the trick begins, the two performers must choose an item in the room, such as a table, to be their "anchor" object. The mind reader knows that the item that the audience selects will be the third thing that the assistant points to after pointing to the anchor.

For example, the performers choose a table as their anchor object. Mind-reading Mom leaves the room, and the members of the audience choose the TV as their object. Mind-reading Mom returns and the trick goes as follows:

Assistant: Is the object I am thinking of the rug on the floor here?

Mind-reading Mom: No.

Assistant: Is it this table? (anchor)

Mind-reading Mom: No.

Assistant: Am I thinking of this chair? (first)

Mind-reading Mom: No.

Assistant: Am I concentrating on this vase? (second)

Mind-reading Mom: No.

Assistant: Is the object I am thinking of this TV? (third)

Mind-reading Mom: Yes, it is.

Great magicians develop a slick and witty banter and put on a dramatic and somewhat over-the-top performance. But what they never, ever do is reveal the secret of how their trick is done.

Sew Much Fun

Learning to sew is a great activity to be enjoyed together and means that you will be able to do any number of craft projects.

RUNNING STITCH

The running stitch is the most basic of stitches and is used for sewing fabric together. If you master this stitch, you will be able to sew almost anything. To secure your stitches, begin and end your sewing with a couple of stitches on top of each other.

Push a threaded needle through the front side of the fabric. Then push it through from the back, leaving an 1/8-inch gap. Continue. On each side of the fabric, there should be stitches of even length, each separated by the same length of space. For heavier fabrics, stitches should be smaller; for lighter fabrics, the stitches can be slightly bigger.

BACKSTITCH

The backstitch is the strongest sewing technique and will look like a continuous line of stitches, like the ones you would get from a sewing machine.

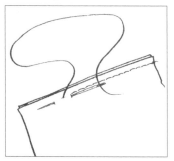

Secure your thread and then do the first stitch as you would for the running stitch. As the needle pushes through to the front of the fabric, instead of going forward, bring the needle back to the end of the previous stitch and push through again. Then bring the needle through at the same distance in front of the finished stitch, pulling it back to stitch over the space once more.

HEMSTITCH

This is a clever stitch that you can't see from the front of the fabric. It is great for sewing hems and cuffs.

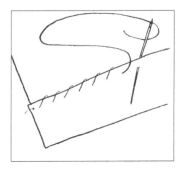

Secure your thread as before, this time sewing your stitches in the hem and not through the main part of the fabric. Working from right to left, pass the needle through the hem and pick up some strands at the back of the main fabric, just above the hem's edge. Be careful not to push the needle all the way through, otherwise the stitching will show, then pass the needle back through the hem. Repeat by picking up a few strands of the main fabric with your needle as before.

Make a Piñata Pig

A piñata is a colorful papier-mâché figure that is filled with candy and small toys. It's usually hung from a tree where children can take turns hitting it until the candy falls out. It's a great idea for children's parties.

Although many people associate the tradition with Mexico, it actually began as a Chinese custom and was introduced to the West by the explorer Marco Polo.

You will need to allow time for drying, so start making your piñata about a week before the party.

You will need:

- a balloon • 5 paper cups, cut in half • 1 large bowl
- 1 cup flour • 4 cups water • newspapers
- candies or small toys • sticky tape
- pink poster paint • a paintbrush
- paper for ears • a black marker
- strong string (about 6 feet)
- a stick for hitting

Blow up a balloon as large as possible.

Tape the bottom halves of four cups onto the balloon body for legs and one to the pointed end of the balloon for the pig's snout.

To make the glue, mix the flour with the water in a large bowl.

Tear the newspaper into strips and dunk them one at a time into your glue mix. Run the strip between two fingers to remove extra glue. Smooth the gluey paper over the balloon pig, overlapping them slightly until everything is covered.

Allow this layer to dry before starting another. Aim for three to six layers depending on how easily you'd like the piñata to break. (The more layers you add, the harder it will be to break.)

When it's dry, cut a flap in the back. Pop and remove the balloon and fill the pig with candy before taping the flap shut.

Paint the pig pink. Cut two ear-shaped pieces out of paper and paint. Then glue them to the head and draw on the pig's features.

Finally, tie the string around the pig's tummy, then loop the ends over a branch or any convenient spot. Make sure the pig hangs low enough for the smallest kids to reach.

Everyone should take turns whacking the piñata until it breaks, spilling its contents. You could offer a prize to the piñata champion, but it's probably best to share the candy among all contestants.

Make a Lavender Sachet

These fragrant little sachets can be placed in drawers to make clothes smell sweet, in the water for a scented bath, or under your pillow. Lavender is thought to aid relaxation and sleep.

You will need:

- fresh or dried lavender
- fine cotton material (muslin or cotton voile are perfect)
- a needle and strong thread
- extra decorations such as embroidered flowers or lace (optional) • a ribbon

If you pick fresh lavender, place the stems on a wire rack until completely dry. Then transfer them into a paper bag and store in a warm place. If possible, space the stems out so they are not touching. Leave the lavender for about a week and then strip the flower heads from the stems.

While waiting for the lavender to dry, cut the cotton material into two squares measuring 6 inches by 6 inches.

With the front of the two panels facing each other, stitch around three sides of the square using a backstitch (see page 15). Leave the top side open.

Fold over a small hem of 1/2 inch at the top and neatly sew using a hemstitch (see page 16). Turn your bag the right side out and sew on any extra decorations you would like to add.

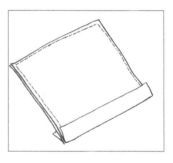

Fill the bag with lavender. Then, using a loose running stitch (see page 14), sew up the final side 1 inch from the top of the bag. As you stitch, pull the thread taut to produce a gathered look.

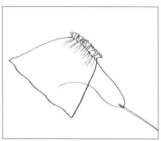

When you have finished stitching, pull the thread taut once more and tie it off.

Add a ribbon around the gathered top of your bag and tie into a bow.

Create a Modern Masterpiece

BEAUTIFUL BLOW PICTURES

Blow painting makes really interesting pictures. It is particularly good for creating tree scenes.

You will need:

• paper • drinking straws • runny, water-based paint
• water to dilute paint

Dilute the paint until it is watery, then put a few drops onto the paper. For trees, put the drops of paint at the

bottom of the page. Using the straw, blow the paint until you have achieved a pattern you like.

Turn the paper around and repeat with a different color. Whatever you do, remember you have to blow, not suck. Keep going with more colors, until the picture is complete, and then leave to dry.

PAINTING WITH MARBLES

Paint-covered marbles will make great patterns on a plain sheet of paper. Be warned though — it can get messy.

You will need:
• white paper • scissors
• a large basin or deep tray
• different colored craft paints in small containers
• a few marbles • plastic spoons

Cut the paper to fit into the base of the basin or tray and place it at the bottom.

Coat a marble with paint by dropping it into one of the paint-filled containers. Lift it out using a spoon and drop it onto the paper. Tilt the basin or tray in different directions so the marble leaves a colorful trail.

Repeat with different colored paints until you have a pattern all over the paper. When the picture is finished, remove from the basin and leave to dry.

How to Customize a T-shirt

Calling all hippy chicks and surfer dudes! If you have an old white T-shirt that you never wear, here are two great ways to give it new life.

TIE-DYE

A tie-dyed T-shirt is eye-catching but simple to achieve.

You will need:

- a white or light-colored cotton T-shirt or top
- a bowl (keep in mind you won't be able to use it for food again) • rubber bands or pieces of string
- a bucket • cold water • hot water
- cold-water dye and cold dye fix
- 6 tablespoons salt • rubber gloves
- an old wooden spoon or tongs
- an old towel or dishtowel
- marbles (optional)

Plan your design. For example, do you want small patterns in one area, or large circles all over? You can even have stripes. Look at the different ideas on pages 26 and 27.

Dampen the T-shirt by submerging it in warm water, then squeeze out the excess. If it is a new shirt, wash it first.

To create tie-dye circles, gather large or small bunches of fabric and twist rubber bands or tie the pieces of string tightly around the bottom of each bunch.

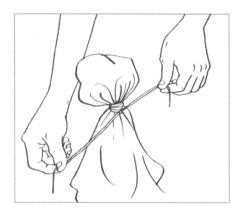

Put the bucket in the sink or bathtub and pour in half a gallon of cold water. Pour 2 cups of hot water into a bowl and mix in the dye. Pour the dye mixture into the bucket and wash the bowl. Pour another 2 cups of hot water into the bowl and mix it with the dye fix and the salt. Stir until all of the salt has dissolved and then pour the mixture into the bucket. Wearing rubber gloves, submerge the T-shirt into the diluted dye and stir slowly with the spoon or tongs for ten minutes. Poke the cloth to keep it submerged.

Leave the T-shirt in the bucket for an hour, stirring occasionally. Take out and rinse under cold water until the water runs clear.

Squeeze the shirt and then roll it in the towel or dishtowel to remove excess water. Now take off the bands and marvel at the cool tie-dye effect.

Tip from Mom: You may be eager to try out your new look, but you'll have to wash and dry the T-shirt first unless you want to end up with green skin!

DIFFERENT PATTERNS

Marble Effect. For an allover marbled effect, scrunch up the T-shirt and tie string or fasten rubber bands around it in a random fashion before dying.

Concentric Circles. For concentric circles (circles within circles) pinch an area of fabric and then use several rubber bands spaced at regular intervals along the length of the fabric. You can do one big bull's-eye pattern or a few smaller ones by using as many bands as you like.

Sunburst. Use marbles to create a different effect. For a sunburst pattern, wrap some material around a marble and then fix several rubber bands around the bunched fabric below, 1/2 inch or so apart.

Stripes. For stripes, roll your T-shirt from top to bottom, like a sausage, as shown. Then place the rubber bands at intervals along the material.

BATIK T-SHIRT

Batik is thought to date back more than 2,000 years, but its exact origins are unknown. Batik is most common in Java and Bali, in Indonesia, where it was once the mark of wealth, position, and even royalty.

Traditionally, designs are achieved with the use of hot wax, but to keep creative fingers from burning, here is a safer alternative. However, you will need patience, as well as a few days to spare.

You will need:

- 1 sheet of thick paper • a pencil • scissors
- 1/3 cup flour • 1/2 cup water
- 1 sheet of cardboard (the side of a cereal box will do)
- a white or light-colored cotton T-shirt
- cold-water dye • a paintbrush
- empty dishwashing liquid or squeeze bottle

First plan your design. Try it on rough paper, coloring it in to see what the T-shirt will look like. Remember to think about color — if you are painting red dye on a yellow T-shirt, for example, it may look orange.

Cut the paper to the shape and size you want the design to be (e.g., square or circular). Sketch your design on the paper, then cut it into a stencil. The flour paste needs to go into the holes, so don't make your design too detailed or it will be difficult to cut out.

Mix the flour and water together. Pour the mixture into the squeeze bottle and replace the cap. Slip the cardboard between the front and back of the T-shirt to protect the fabric behind your design.

Lay the stencil on the front of the T-shirt and carefully squeeze the flour paste into the holes. The areas covered in glue will be the ones that stay the same color as the T-shirt. Now squeeze the paste around the edge of the stencil — this will keep the dye from running out of the border.

Carefully remove the stencil and leave the mixture to dry. This can take up to two days, so be patient.

When the T-shirt is completely dry, mix some cold-water dye according to the instructions on the package.

Paint over your design using the brush. Be careful not to leave any gaps and not to go outside the border of your design. Leave the T-shirt to dry for another day.

When your design is completely dry, carefully peel off the paste and wash the T-shirt. Finally, you can wear your unique T-shirt with pride.

Animal Magic with Cards

If you like playing Snap, you will love this card game with some extra animal chaos thrown in. The object of the game is to be the player left with all the cards.

You will need:

• a deck of cards • pen and paper • a bowl

Each player chooses an animal and writes it down on a scrap of paper. The animals' names should be as long or hard to say as possible, such as gnu or hippopotamus. Put the pieces of paper in the bowl, and each player then picks one out and shows it to everyone else.

The cards are then dealt into piles, facedown until the pack is gone. Players are not allowed to look at their cards.

The player to the left of the dealer turns his or her top card over to start a faceup pile. The other players do the same, one by one. This continues until a player spots that another player has a card with the same number or picture as his or her own. That player must then shout out the name of the other player's animal three times.

If a player shouts out the correct animal and in a way that doesn't jumble the name, he or she wins the other player's faceup pile. If he or she gets it wrong, that player must give his or her own faceup pile to the other player.

The winner is the player left with all the cards.

The Shopping List Game

This game is a great memory tester. Players work their way through the alphabet, taking turns completing the sentence "I went shopping and I bought . . ."

The first player might say, "I went shopping and I bought an apple."

The next player would then repeat this sentence, adding an item begining with *b*.

For example: "I went shopping and I bought an apple and a basketball."

Keep taking turns, repeating the sentence and the list of items that have been bought so far, and adding another item to the end of the list.

If someone forgets an item, lists the items in the wrong order, or pauses for longer than a count of five, he or she is out. The winner is the person who stays in the game the longest.

Tip from Mom: This game can also be played with the sentence "I am going to a party and I am going to bring . . ."

A Spa Day Treat for Mom

When Mother's Day or Mom's birthday rolls around, what could be more special than creating her own personal health spa at home? There's no need to spend money on expensive skin-care products – you can make your own from the contents of the kitchen cupboard and fridge.

Put on Mom's favorite CD of relaxing music and tell her to put on her robe. It's time for her to relax.

Warning: If Mom can't eat any of the following ingredients because of an allergy, don't spread it on her skin!

OATMEAL AND HONEY FACE MASK

You will need:

• 1 egg • 1/3 cup oatmeal • 3 tablespoons honey

Crack an egg over a bowl, keeping the yolk in one half of the shell. Pass the yolk from one half of the shell to the other, letting the white slip into the bowl below. When the shell contains just the yolk, place it in another bowl and save the white to use for something else.

Add the rest of the ingredients to the egg yolk and stir until they are thoroughly mixed.

Use a paintbrush to apply the mixture to Mom's face, using a circular motion. Be careful to avoid the eye area.

Then tell Mom to sit back and relax for ten minutes. When the time is up, rinse off the face mask with warm water.

BANANA AND HONEY FACE MASK

Use a fork to mash a ripe banana in a bowl. Add a teaspoon of honey and mix together well.

STRAWBERRY FACE MASK

Mash four large strawberries and spread the pulp onto the skin.

COOLING CUCUMBER AND YOGURT FACE MASK

Purée a quarter of a cucumber in a blender and mix with a tablespoon of plain yogurt.

OLIVE OIL AND OATMEAL SCRUB

You will need:

- 2 tablespoons oatmeal
- 1 tablespoon olive oil
- 1 tablespoon lemon juice
- 1 tablespoon brown sugar
- 1 teaspoon honey

Mix the ingredients together in a bowl and apply to Mom's face with firm circular movements. Rinse off with warm water.

AVOCADO AND BANANA SCRUB

You will need:

- 1 dried avocado pit (left to dry for three days or more beforehand)
- a plastic bag • a hammer
- 1/2 ripe banana • 1 tablespoon olive oil

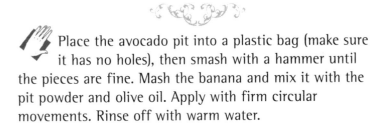 Place the avocado pit into a plastic bag (make sure it has no holes), then smash with a hammer until the pieces are fine. Mash the banana and mix it with the pit powder and olive oil. Apply with firm circular movements. Rinse off with warm water.

Tip from Mom: After all these treatments, Mom should splash her face with cold water to close the pores, and then pat dry with a clean towel.

Make a Dream Catcher

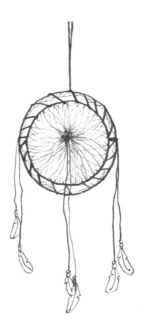

Native Americans believed that dreams traveled through the air before reaching sleepers. They hung dream catchers up to stop bad dreams from coming their way. The nightmares got caught in the webs, while the good dreams slid off the feathers at the bottom and dropped softly onto the sleepers below.

You will need:

- a round plastic lid from an ice cream container
- a craft knife • a mesh fruit or vegetable bag
- a bobby pin • colored yarn

- scissors • beads • craft glue
- colored feathers (available at craft shops and some supermarkets)

Cut out the middle of the ice cream container lid, leaving the rim. This can be done with scissors, but it might be easier with a craft knife.

Pull the netting tightly over the rim, then tie together at the back.

Using the bobby pin as a needle, wind the yarn tightly around the outside of the hoop and through the mesh until the rim is covered. Then tie the ends of the yarn together. Tie a loop of yarn to the top of the hoop to hang it up.

Cut away the rough ends of the netting at the back of your dream catcher using scissors.

Cut three strands of yarn, about 2 feet long, for the beads. Double the strands over and tie the folded ends to the sides and middle of the dream catcher. Make sure the loose ends hang down. Then add your beads. Tie a large knot in the yarn to keep the beads on.

Now glue a feather to the bottom of each strand.

The dream catcher needs to be suspended within a few feet of the bed and able to move freely. If possible, it is best to hang it from the ceiling. Sweet dreams!

Grow Froggy Friends

Collecting frog eggs and raising tiny black tadpoles until they are little jumping froglets is a fascinating springtime activity that brings the magic of nature into your home.

You will need:

• a fishing net • a bucket
• a fish tank with a lid • fish food flakes

Start checking local ponds for frog spawn, or large masses of eggs, in early spring. When you find a pond with lots of spawn, use a net to scoop out a small isolated clump. Be careful not to break up a large clump or the delicate eggs inside could get damaged.

Transfer the frog spawn into a bucket filled with water from the pond. Add some pondweed. The young tadpoles will eat this as they grow, and it will help to oxygenate the water.

Fill the fish tank with tap water and dechlorinate it by leaving it outside for a few days to settle. Alternatively, use a chemical bought from a local pet store. Follow the instructions on the packaging. It is important to do this because tap water contains chemicals that can kill tadpoles.

Carefully transfer the frog spawn and pondweed to the tank. Now wait patiently for the wiggling tadpoles to emerge.

Watch the frog spawn closely as the days pass. The small black dots will grow larger and elongate as the tadpoles grow inside the eggs. When they emerge, the new tiny tadpoles won't be very exciting at first. They do not eat and they stay very close to the clump of spawn, getting their nutrients from their empty egg.

As they get larger, they will move about more and begin to feed on the weed taken from their home pond. Eventually they will sprout gills at the sides of their heads to get oxygen from the water, and their bodies will fatten.

After about a week or so, front legs will begin to grow and the tadpoles will begin to crave a more meaty diet. Fish food flakes are good for this, but be careful not to add too many or the water will get very dirty. Adding a bit more pond water at this stage will also give them a little natural food.

As their tails shrink and their back legs begin to grow, the tadpoles will want to get out on land. Put a rock in the tank so that they are able to climb out above water level and breathe with their newly developed lungs. Note that their gills will have completely disappeared. Now that the frogs are on the move, it is time to set them free.

Take your little froglets back to the pond they came from, or they will be hopping mad.

Great Avocado Ghouls

These tasty, nutritious treats look pretty scary, and are ideal for Halloween, but they taste heavenly enough for any day of the year.

You will need:

- 2 ripe avocados • 1/2 lemon
- 6 ounces canned tuna
- 4 pitted black olives
- 8 capers • 1 tomato

Cut the avocados in half and remove the pits. Scrape the flesh into a large bowl, without damaging the skin. Squeeze the juice of half a lemon into the bowl with the avocado flesh. This will make your ghouls taste delicious and it will also keep the flesh from turning brown.

Drain the tuna, then add it to the mixture in the bowl. Mash together until thoroughly mixed and then spoon into the empty avocado skins. Press down until the tops are smooth.

Cut the olives in half and place two pieces on each avocado half for eyes. Add a caper to each eye as a pupil. Slice the tomato and use half a slice to make each ghoul's gruesome smile.

For an easy vegetarian version of this dish, leave out the tuna and mix in some finely chopped tomatoes instead, to make a guacamole filling.

Tip from Mom: Ghouls can come in many shapes and delicious disguises. Why not create your own terrifying taste sensations? You could use small chunks of pepper for scary red eyes or bits of radish for frightening fangs.

Have a Freaky Friday

Freaky Friday is a classic movie about Tess Coleman, a stylish single mother (played by Jamie Lee Curtis), and her rock-chick daughter Anna Coleman (played by Lindsay Lohan), who switch places for a whole day. If you haven't seen this film, then watching it is a great "thing to do with Mom."

What would it be like to switch places in real life? What if Mom suddenly had to do homework again or go to bed at a certain time? Or what if the kids were in charge, and could decide what was for dinner or how much TV they were allowed to watch?

Have your own Freaky Friday, Thursday, Sunday, or any other day and find out.

THE SWAP

Mom, take a look through your closet and see what outfits are most like something a child would wear. Loud T-shirts and jeans are best for this. Jeans should be rolled up to give a more youthful look. Or you could try to fashion some kind of school uniform. Take special care to adopt any peculiarities of your child's speech, such as using two syllables to say mom — "Oh, M-om!"

Kids, think about how Mom speaks. If she has any embarrassing pet names for you, such as Sweet Pea or Snookums, you can now call her these names for the whole game and see how much she likes it.

THE GAME

There are no rules for this game apart from acting like each other. Let your imaginations run wild. Mom may not want to do homework when she is told to and may go and turn on the TV. Kids may want the family to have ice cream and cake for dinner.

Make sure you remember to swap back again before it's time for school or you could get some very strange looks.

Make a Spectacular Fireworks Display Picture

Fireworks displays can be great fun, but it can be tricky to take a really good photograph of fireworks — blink and you will miss them. With these pictures, you can get inspiration from your next local display and then come home and make some spectacular displays of your own.

You will need:

• a sheet of paper • colored pens or pencils
• a large black crayon • a pen cap or small coin
• some sheets of newspaper

Put some sheets of newspaper down to protect the surface you're working on. Now take the pens and start coloring the paper. You want to color the whole sheet — so get to work. Try drawing rainbow stripes, random blobs, connecting squares, or anything you like. Just make sure that every bit of white is covered with all of your favorite colors.

When your paper is fully covered, take your black crayon and scribble over your page until it is all black. Don't hold back, the blacker the better. Remember this is supposed to be the night sky.

When the page is completely covered in black crayon and none of the colors underneath are visible, you're ready to "draw" your picture. Use a small coin or the cap of a pen to scratch into the surface of the black crayon and reveal the bright colors beneath. Add swirls, starbursts, spirals, dots, rocket shapes, and sparklers. Spectacular!

If you make a mistake or you get bored with your picture, just grab your black crayon, darken the picture up, and start again.

Make Petal Perfume

Lots of celebrities have their own signature scents, and you can, too! Girls can wear it themselves and boys can give it as a gift. Hunting for the petals for your very own perfume is the perfect way to spend a long, hot summer's day. Decide together with Mom which flowers to use to avoid destroying your mom or dad's prizewinning dahlias.

CLASSIC ROSE PERFUME

Classic Rose Perfume will smell wonderful for a few days, but it can spoil very quickly. Storing it in the fridge will make it last longer and will also make it cool and refreshing to apply.

You will need:

- rose petals (as many as you can find!)
- 2 clean jars • water

- an attractive glass bottle • dishwashing liquid
  - white vinegar • a strainer

Put the petals into the jar and add enough water to cover them, plus 1/4 inch more. Leave in a warm sunny spot for at least a day.

In the meantime, wash a glass bottle with warm water and dishwashing liquid, then rinse with a solution of water and a few drops of white vinegar. Be careful not to add too much or your perfume could end up smelling like salad dressing!

Strain the petal water into a clean jar, squashing the petals to extract more scent. Pour into the clean bottle.

HEAVENLY BLOSSOM SCENT

This recipe will work well with any fragrant blossoms, but lavender, honeysuckle, and lilac are particularly good. This scent also has the advantage of lasting longer than rose perfume. It will stay fresh for up to a month.

You will need:

- some cheesecloth • a bowl
- 1 cup chopped petals or flowers • 2 cups water
  - a saucepan • a glass bottle • a ribbon

Lay the cheesecloth in the bottom of the bowl so that the edges come over the side. Place the petals into the bowl and add water until the petals are completely submerged. Cover the bowl and leave overnight.

The following day, carefully lift the cheesecloth out of the bowl, drawing the corners in to avoid dropping the petals. Gather up the corners and squeeze the water out of the cheesecloth into a small clean saucepan, adding any water left in the bowl.

Bring the liquid to a boil and then simmer until a small amount of liquid (about a tablespoonful) is left. Remove from the heat and leave to cool.

Pour your scent into the bottle and add a pretty ribbon.

Rustle Up a Leafy Autumn Scene

The vibrant reds, browns, and yellows of autumn leaves make woods and yards look beautiful and can also make a stunning work of art.

Choose a crisp, blue-skied autumn day and go out for a long walk. Leaves can be found just about anywhere there are trees, and nobody minds if you pick them up off the ground. Make sure you dust off any bugs before you put them in your bag.

Collect as many different shapes and colors as you can.

PRESERVING LEAVES
You will need:

- a variety of autumn leaves • waxed paper
- a dishtowel or piece of cloth • an iron
- scissors • acrylic craft spray from a craft shop

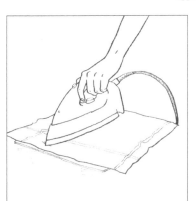

Place the leaves between two sheets of waxed paper and cover with an old dishtowel or piece of cloth.

Iron the fabric with the iron on a warm setting. This will seal the sheets of waxed paper together with the leaves in between.

Cut around the shape of your leaf, leaving a narrow margin of waxed paper around the leaf edge.

Set aside your leaves for a day or two and then spray them with a sealant, such as acrylic craft spray.

PRESSING LEAVES

If you don't have waxed paper, don't despair. You can still preserve the leaves by pressing them between the pages of a large book.

You will need:

- a variety of autumn leaves • some sheets of newspaper
- a large, heavy book • some other books to rest on top

Place each leaf between two sheets of newspaper and press between the pages of the large book.

Leave at least 1/4 inch of book pages between each leaf you press. When the book is full of leaves, shut it and place more books on top for extra pressure.

Leave these for about two weeks and then remove each leaf carefully.

THE PICTURE

When the leaves are ready, you can create a picture. Take a sheet of paper and experiment with where to position the leaves. Some leaves make great fish shapes. When you are happy with your design, stick the leaves down with glue and leave to dry.

Perfect a Picnic *Pan Bagnat*

Pan bagnat literally means "bathed bread" since the bread is bathed in dressing so that it absorbs all of the delicious flavors from the filling.

Pan bagnat is great because people of all ages can prepare it. And, it can be made several hours before you go on a picnic.

There are many variations on the fillings, so you can always experiment, but here are a few suggestions.

TUNA PAN BAGNAT

You will need:

- 1 ciabatta loaf or French bread
- 3 to 4 large tomatoes
- 2 hard-boiled eggs • 8 pitted olives
- 3 tablespoons French dressing • fresh basil leaves
- 3 ounces canned tuna, drained • 2 scallions, chopped
- plastic wrap

Cut the bread lengthwise so that only one side is cut through while the other remains attached. (If using a baguette, cut in half first.) Slice the tomatoes and eggs and cut the olives in half.

Spread the insides of the bread with the dressing and cover with the fresh basil leaves. Layer the rest of the ingredients on top.

Close the loaf and wrap it tightly in plastic wrap. Then chill it in the fridge for at least two hours. Cut into small portions before eating.

PAN BAGNAT PROVENÇAL

You will need:

- 1 very large, round, country-style ciabatta loaf
- 4 ounces pesto • 1/2 cup French dressing
- 5 ounces salami • 4 large tomatoes, sliced
- 10 to 20 pitted olives • 8 slices prosciutto

- 9 ounces fresh basil
- 9 ounces roasted red peppers
- plastic wrap

 If using a round loaf, slice off the top and keep it to serve as a lid. With a ciabatta, slice it lengthwise so that only one side is cut through while the other remains attached.

 Tear out the bread in the center of the loaf, leaving a hollow that's about an inch deep. Using a food processor, make bread crumbs, then mix half of them with the pesto. Mix the other half with the French dressing.

Add two-thirds of the pesto mix to the bottom half of the bread, then layer the salami, tomato, olives, French dressing mixture, prosciutto, basil, peppers, and then the remainder of the pesto mix. Pack everything in and close the *pan bagnat.*

Tightly wrap in plastic wrap and chill in the fridge. When it's time to serve the sandwich, unwrap it and slice into smaller pieces.

 A sharp bread knife is recommended to divide up the loaves.

Play the Letter-chain Game

This is a great way to liven up a long car journey. It is suitable for players of all ages. You can have as many people competing as you like.

Start by picking a category (one that matches the ability of all the players). Younger players might prefer a category such as animals or food. Slightly older players might jump at the chance to name films, celebrities, or countries.

The youngest player starts the game by naming an example of something that fits into the category, such as "dog," if the subject is animals.

The second-youngest player must then name an animal that begins with the last letter of the previous answer. For example: "giraffe," because *g* is the last letter of "dog."

This continues until all players have given an answer in ascending order of age.

If a player gets stumped by his or her letter, he or she is out. The winner is the last person left in the game.

Play can then start again with a whole new subject and a whole new letter chain. Let your imagination run wild!

Tip from Mom: When you've worked your way through all the obvious categories, experiment with a wide range of weird and wacky subjects. How about imaginary creatures or storybook characters?

Super Stained-glass Window Cookies

Here's how to create a stunning piece of edible art inside a cookie. Unleash your imagination as you design your dazzling "windows."

You will need:

- 1/2 cup superfine sugar • 1/2 cup butter or margarine
- 2 cups flour • 1/2 teaspoon vanilla extract
- juice and rind of 1/2 a lemon • 1 egg yolk
- plastic wrap • hard candies in a variety of colors

 Preheat the oven to 400°F.

Grease two baking sheets. Put the butter or margarine and the sugar into a large bowl, and mix together with a wooden spoon. When the mixture is soft and a light-yellow color, add the flour, vanilla extract, grated lemon rind, and the juice. Stir all the ingredients together.

Beat the egg yolk in a small bowl and then add it to the mixture. Combine to make a dough. Cover the dough in plastic wrap and put it in the fridge for at least 25 minutes.

Remove the dough from the fridge and on a very lightly floured surface, roll it out until it is about 1/2-inch thick.

Cut out your cookies using a variety of cookie cutter shapes.

Make a hole in each cookie for a "stained-glass window." Experiment by cutting out various window shapes like squares, hearts, circles, and even triangles. Use mini cookie cutters if you have them. Place the cookies on the baking sheets.

 Put the cookies in the oven and bake for 6 minutes. Then remove from the oven.

Now for the fun part. Place a candy in each of the cutout shapes (being careful not to burn your hands on the hot cookies or baking sheets).

 Put the cookies back in the oven and cook for 4 more minutes or until the candies start to melt. Remove the cookies from the oven. Place on a wire rack and leave to cool.

Take a step back and admire your stained-glass treats.

Tip from Mom:
Stained-glass window cookies make beautiful Christmas tree decorations. Make a hole in the top of each one before baking. When the cookies have cooled, thread ribbon through the holes and hang them on your tree.

Make a Luxurious Gift for Grandma

This beautiful bath puff is perfect for your grandma. It looks lovely and she'll find it very useful at bath time for soap or shower gel.

Choose a pretty color of netting and a matching ribbon to create a great gift.

You will need:

- 3 feet soft tulle or netting • pins
- a needle with a large eye
- thread in a color to match the tulle
- scissors • 20 inches pretty ribbon

Spread the netting out flat. Fold the fabric over 5 inches up from the bottom edge. Fold over again and again until all the tulle has been folded into a tube that's 5 inches wide.

Secure the fabric with pins, and then sew along the center of the tube from one end to the other using a running stitch (see page 14).

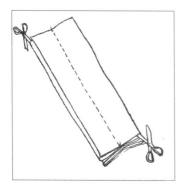

Once you have sewn along the length of the tulle, cut along both edges.

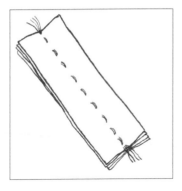

Using a loose running stitch, sew along the length of the tulle again, without securing your stitches at the end. The thread needs to be very strong for this so try quadrupling your thread (so that you are sewing with four strands instead of one).

Pull on the thread so that the tulle gathers together in a long ruffle. Secure at the end with a few stitches.

Finally stitch the two ends together to form a loop.

Attach the ribbon to the puff so it can be hung up to dry after use.

Now all you need to do is wrap it up with a bottle of bubble bath and present it with a kiss to your lucky grandma.

Twenty Questions

In this game one player thinks of an animal, plant, or object, and the other players must try to guess what it is by asking a maximum of twenty questions.

Each question can only be answered with a "yes" or a "no." For example, you must not ask "How many legs does it have?" but you may ask "Does it have four legs?"

If the correct answer is guessed within the allotted number of questions, the person who guessed wins the round and it is his or her turn to think of something.

Ornamental Eggshell Planter

When filled with watercress, these planters are a great feature for a windowsill or a miniature garden (see pages 2 to 5). They also act as a miniature kitchen garden for Mom to place on the windowsill, as the watercress is delicious in sandwiches and salads.

You will need:

• 2 eggs • a knife
• 2 old egg cups (preferably matching)
• absorbent cotton balls • watercress seeds • acrylic paints

Boil the eggs for 4 minutes. Then, using a knife, remove the tops about one-third of the way down. Scoop out the insides and serve with toast.

Carefully wash the eggshells to remove any lingering egg bits and leave to dry.

Put the eggshells in the egg cups — open side up — and decorate them using acrylic paint (acrylic paint is waterproof when dry and will prevent your design from running). Paint your eggs white or pale gray for a Grecian effect, or use a warm terra-cotta color to give your planters a modern Mediterranean feel.

Leave the eggshells to dry, and then remove them from the cups. Paint the egg cups to match your eggs.

When the egg cups are dry, pop in the shells — open side up. Put enough absorbent cotton into each planter so that it comes to about 1/2 inch from the top. Add just enough water to soak the cotton.

Sprinkle the wet cotton with watercress seeds. Then place the finished planters in your miniature garden or on your windowsill.

Wait for the watercress to sprout — this should take up to a week. Keep watering your planters so that they don't dry out.

Create a Moving Card

Pop-up cards are a lot of fun, and with this one the little chick opens and shuts its beak as if it's really tweeting! They are perfect for Easter or, for a Christmas variation, you could draw a cardinal in a snowy scene. You could draw a croaking frog or even a friend who likes to talk a lot.

You will need:

- 2 pieces of construction paper in different colors
- glue • scissors
- markers, pencils, or crayons

Fold one piece of construction paper in half. Cut a line about 2 inches long across the middle of the crease.

Fold back each of the flaps to make two triangles, leaving a triangular hole at the crease. Sharpen the folds by running a fingernail along the folded edge of each triangle.

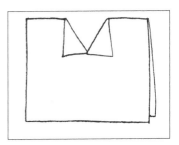

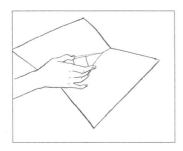

Unfold the triangles and open the card about halfway.

Push one of the triangles through the hole and pinch to make it stand up. Repeat with the other triangle.

Close the card and press down on the folds to strengthen the creases. The "beak" should now pop up when you open the card.

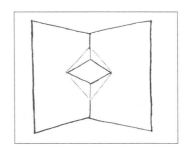

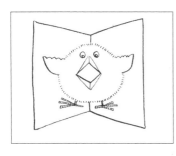

Fold the second piece of construction paper and dab some glue around the inside edges. Stick the new piece to the back of your pop-up card, making sure none of the glue goes near the beak.

Now draw your bird around the beak and write your message.

Launch Orange Jell-O Boats

Liven up dessert with a fantastic fleet of orange Jell-O boats. For the perfect party treat, just add ice cream.

You will need:

- 3 oranges • 1 package fruit Jell-O
- 8 toothpicks • rice paper

Make the Jell-O with hot and cold water, following the instructions on the package. To make a firmer Jell-O, use 3/4 of the water suggested on the package. Leave to cool until it is lukewarm. You can speed this up by adding a few ice cubes, or placing it in the refrigerator.

Meanwhile, cut the oranges in half using a sharp knife, and begin to loosen their insides by cutting around the inside edges. Be very careful not to pierce the skin of the orange or you won't be able to pour Jell-O into them.

Scoop out the rest of the insides of the orange halves using a spoon, trying to remove as much as possible.

Keep the empty orange halves steady by placing them in a pan, then fill each one to the top with Jell-O. Put the pan containing your oranges in the fridge to set.

Make the sails while waiting for your Jell-O boats to set. Cut triangles about 2 1/2 inches high out of the rice paper and thread with toothpicks to act as masts.

When the Jell-O has set, cut the oranges again so that they are now in quarters. Arrange them on a plate (a blue one is best) or cover a plate with foil so it looks like glistening waves.

You are now ready to put up your sails and drift into the sunset.

Play the Category Game

This is a great game to play with a small group.

Each player needs a sheet of paper and a pen. Divide the paper into a grid, with eleven boxes down the left-hand side and two columns wide enough to write four or five words in. At the top of the left-hand column write "Category" and at the top of the right-hand column write "Word."

Each player picks a category and all players write them into the boxes in the left-hand column. Typical categories include TV shows, authors, pop stars, trees, flowers, etc.

When ten categories are filled in, a letter is picked at random by someone sticking a pencil into the page of a newspaper, magazine, or book with his or her eyes closed. Whichever letter the pencil is either touching or nearest to is the chosen letter for the round.

Timing with a watch or timer, one player says, "Go." Players now have two minutes to fill in as many of the categories as they can with answers beginning with the chosen letter.

Where the answer is a person's name, the last name should begin with the correct letter.

Here is an example of what the sheet may look like when the chosen letter is *S*.

CATEGORY	WORD
Trees	Sycamore
Pop stars	Britney Spears
Movie stars	Sylvester Stallone
Authors	William Shakespeare
Books	*Sense and Sensibility*
Cities	San Diego
Countries	Spain
Animals	Sheep
TV shows	*Sesame Street*
Flowers	Sunflower

If anyone fills in their sheet before the two minutes are up, they can shout "stop" and the round ends. Otherwise all players must stop writing after two minutes.

Scores are determined by the number of people who have the same answer as you for each category. The top score is ten, but one point is knocked off for each person who duplicates your answer. For example, if three people have the answer "Spain," each player only scores seven for that answer.

A new letter is then chosen for the next round.

Make Your Own Lemonade

On a hot summer's day, there's nothing more refreshing than a large pitcher of homemade lemonade.

You will need:

- 7 lemons (to make a slightly sweeter drink, replace one of the lemons with a large orange)
- 1 1/2 cups sugar
- 6 cups water • honey to taste

Grate the zest of two of the lemons into a large saucepan. Pour in 6 cups of water and add the sugar.

 Heat the lemon zest, water, and sugar mixture until all of the sugar has dissolved and leave to cool.

Squeeze the juice of all the lemons into a large jug. Pour the cooled sugar water over the lemon juice and stir.

Each time you make lemonade, the flavor will be slightly different, so always taste the mixture before serving. Stir in a teaspoon of honey if necessary. Add some ice cubes to the pitcher and serve.

Tip from Mom: To make pink lemonade, add a cup of cranberry juice. This will give your drink a nice tang and it will make it a fun color.

Make a Denim Bag

Denim bags are great — lightweight, washable, and stylish. Instead of paying a fortune for one in a store, find an old pair of jeans and recycle them into this must-have accessory. Make sure nobody wants the jeans, though — you don't want to take the scissors to Mom's or Dad's new designer denim!

You will need:

• an old pair of jeans • a ruler • chalk or a pen
• scissors • a brightly colored cotton or silk scarf
• optional embellishments

Zip up the jeans and turn them inside out. Lay them out flat in front of you, bottom side up, and measure 1 inch down the inseam.

With chalk, draw a line across the leg at this mark and repeat for the other leg. Cut the legs off at the line you have drawn.

Sew each leg closed 1 inch from the cut edge. Trim the seam to 1/2 inch, then turn the bag so it is right side out.

To make a handle, thread a brightly colored scarf through the belt loops and tie the ends together. Alternatively, cut the two inseams from the leftover legs of the jeans and sew onto both sides of the bag to make long handles.

Now add any embellishments you like, such as fabric patches, buttons, or ribbons. Stitch them into place for a truly original design.

Make Chocolate Leaves

Chocolate leaves make impressive and delicious decorations for cakes or desserts.

You will need:

- nontoxic leaves such as rose, lemon, or bay leaves
- a dishtowel • some sheets of newspaper
- 4 ounces semisweet chocolate
- a glass bowl • a pastry brush • waxed paper
- a shallow baking pan or rolling pin

Carefully wash the leaves, then pat them dry using a clean dishtowel.

Cover your work surface with a sheet of newspaper to protect it from any stray dribbles of chocolate, and lay some waxed paper on a tray for the leaves.

Break the chocolate into chunks in a glass bowl.

Melt the chocolate either on low power in the microwave, or over a pan of boiling water, stirring until it is liquid.

When the chocolate has melted, remove it from the heat. Use a table knife or pastry brush to spread a thick and even layer of chocolate on the underside (the bumpy side) of each leaf. Be careful not to go over the edges or your leaves will be difficult to peel off later.

Place the leaves, chocolate side up, on the pan lined with waxed paper or over a rolling pin to give them a nice curl. Put them in the fridge for about an hour.

Take the leaves out of the fridge. Holding the stalk, gently peel the leaf away from the chocolate. Don't worry if some of your leaves break at this stage. With patience and practice you will have forests of them!

Refrigerate the chocolate leaves in an airtight container until you're ready to enjoy them!

Fancy Butterfly Magnets

Use coffee filters to make the multicolored wings of a butterfly. The resulting butterflies can be made into fridge magnets or brooches, or clipped onto curtains.

You will need:

- food coloring in various colors
- clean yogurt containers (or any small containers)
- water • a round coffee filter • a cake pan
- an eyedropper or small paintbrush • black or brown paint
- pipe cleaners • a wooden clothespin • strong glue
- small magnet or magnetic strip, or safety pin (for brooch)

In the yogurt containers, mix six drops of food coloring with a few drops of water (make sure you don't dilute it too much).

Put a coffee filter in the bottom of a cake pan. Using the eyedropper or paintbrush, drip the colored water onto the filter, allowing it to spread.

Do the same with another color, then another, and so on, making different colored blobs all over the paper. Leave to dry.

Paint the clothespin black or brown and leave to dry.

Fold a pipe cleaner into a V-shape and glue to the flat end of the clothespin (the part you pinch). This forms the antennae of the butterfly.

Scrunch the filter in the middle, to form wings, and then clip the clothespin onto the middle. Gently pull the paper into wing shapes.

Glue magnetic tape or a magnet to the back of your butterfly and stick it on the fridge. Alternatively, attach a safety pin using sticky tape to make a brooch.

If you can't find any safety pins, clip the clothespin to your curtains.

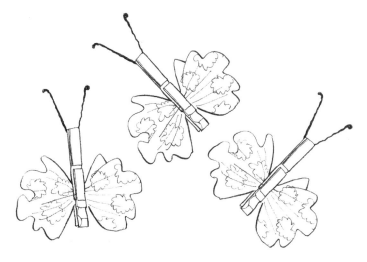

Pasta and Rice Pictures

Raid the cupboard and create exciting pictures. Pasta and rice with an added dash of color make great materials for getting creative, but it can get messy. Put a mat or some old newspaper down before you start.

You will need:

• rice • pasta of various shapes (farfalle [bows], elbow macaroni, fusilli [twists], and penne [tubes] all work well) • a resealable plastic bag • food coloring • bowls • some sheets of newspaper • paper • craft glue • a pen or pencil

Place some of the pasta in a resealable plastic bag with a few drops of food coloring. Seal the bag, shake, and then spread the pasta onto newspaper to dry. Don't shake so hard that you break the pasta pieces — just shake enough to spread the color around.

Repeat with as many different colors and pasta shapes as you wish.

To color the rice, divide it into various bowls (margarine tubs or old yogurt containers will work as well) and then add a drop or two of food coloring into each. Stir thoroughly. Add more food coloring if you want to increase the strength of the color. Spread the rice out on newspaper to dry.

Put the colored pasta and rice into separate bowls in the middle of your kitchen table.

Draw a picture and then glue on the pasta shapes and rice. If you prefer you could skip the drawing stage and just go with the flow in the tradition of all great abstract artists.

Leave the paper flat until the glue is dry to prevent your picture from falling off the page.

Be careful! Even when they are dry, these works of art tend to shed the odd pasta bow and sprinkle rice on the carpet.

Make a Haunted House

Get crafty at Halloween and create your very own haunted house. It's a perfect way to spook visitors and have a little October fun.

You will need:

• an empty shoe box • scissors
• a sizable lump of modeling clay • a sharp pencil
• a ruler • black poster paint • a paintbrush
• white tissue paper • sticky tape • cotton thread

Cut away one end of the shoe box completely, saving the piece of cardboard for later on.

Position the opposite end of the box over the piece of modeling clay and use the point of a pencil to make a hole in the middle of the cardboard.

Paint the inside of the box black and leave it to dry.

Cut out an oblong piece of tissue paper, slightly larger than the end of the box, and tape it over the open end.

Sketch the shape of a bat, a ghost, and a cat on the spare piece of cardboard from the end of the shoe box. Cut them out and paint them black. Put them aside to dry.

When dry, use the pencil to make a hole in the top of each of your scary shapes, pushing through the cardboard into the modeling clay underneath. In the same way, make three holes on each of the long sides of the shoe box in the positions shown.

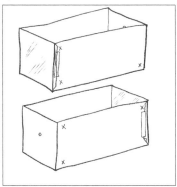

Measure and cut two pieces of thread that are twice as long as the width of the box and one piece that is twice the length of the box. Thread the longest piece of thread through the top of the bat and secure with a knot in the center. Then repeat with the cat and ghost pieces.

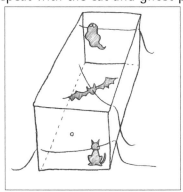

Thread the cat between the two lowest holes at the front of the shoe box and then string the ghost between the two highest holes at the back. Lastly, thread the bat diagonally across the box between the remaining holes.

Tie a loop at each end of the pieces of thread and use them to pull the spooky characters back and forth inside the box. Replace the lid.

Place your haunted house near a good source of light. A window is fine during the day, or a lamp will work in the evening. Now choose a victim and creep them out by getting them to look through the spy hole while you pull the characters back and forth. You could even make up scary stories to tell while you do it.

Make a Super Ponytail Holder

Use the brand-new sewing skills you learned on pages 14 to 16 to make a fabulous hair accessory. Making your own accessories means you can match them exactly to your outfit. Fabric ponytail holders are great to make as gifts or to sell at a school craft fair.

You will need:

- a piece of fabric (17 inches by 5 inches)
- needle and thread • 2 safety pins
- elastic (1/4 inch by 10 inches)

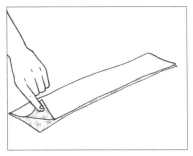

Fold the fabric over along the long side, so that only the underside shows.

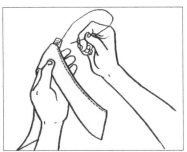

Using the backstitch (see page 15) sew along the open edge about 1/2 inch in. Turn the fabric tube right side out.

Pin one of the safety pins to the end of the elastic and attach it to one end of the tube.

Pin the other safety pin to the opposite end of the elastic and thread the elastic through the tube.

Undo the safety pins without letting go of the two ends of the elastic, then tie a secure knot, leaving 2 inches of elastic at the ends. Tuck the ends inside the material. Fold over the cut edges of the fabric. Sew the two ends of the fabric tube together.

Host a Clothes-swap Party

Everyone has clothes in their closet they have outgrown or never wear. However, one person's fashion disaster is another's fashion find of the century. Why not clear out and refresh your wardrobe by hosting a clothes-swap party? Hand-me-downs are nowhere near as horrible if they come from that cool, older kid from down the street.

You will need:

• invitations • guests • party food and drinks
• paper (in three different colors)

Pick a date and write out invitations a few weeks beforehand. Here is an example, but you can word it however you wish:

Dear ....

We have decided it is time for a wardrobe makeover and were hoping you could help. Please join us for an evening of fashion exchange, fun, and food on (insert date).

Please bring at least five items of clothing that you are ready to swap. All items must be clean and in good condition.

The clothes swap will begin at 7 P.M.

RSVP: (Insert your names/phone number).

When the day of the party arrives, work together to prepare drinks and snacks. You also need to prepare the room for the swap. Create three areas for clothes. For example, you can divide them into tops, bottoms, and accessories. If there are few accessories, substitute those for shoes, or whichever three categories you think will give the most equal distribution. If you want, you could also divide adults' and children's clothing. Give each area its own ticket color.

When your guests arrive, make sure you put their coats in another room so they don't end up being part of the swap. Have your guests put their swap clothes into the appropriate areas. Write a ticket out for each item and person. For example, if tops are in the yellow area, and your guest adds a top to the pile, write your guest's name on a yellow ticket.

Put all the tickets into a large bowl and shake them up. Then take turns picking tickets out of the bowl. The person whose name is on the ticket can then choose an item from the appropriate colored pile. For example, if your yellow ticket is picked, you can choose a top from the pile in the yellow area.

Tip from Mom: To add a bit more excitement to the proceedings, add the following rule. If an item is chosen, and another person wants it, he or she can raise a hand and say "I object." A game of Rock Paper Scissors or a coin toss can then be used to determine who gets the item.

Make sure your friends know all the rules before you begin swapping, and explain that some people may end up with a few things they don't want, as this is the nature of the swap. These can be collected at the end of the party, bagged, and donated to a local charity.

Plan the Perfect Picnic

What could be more fun on a bright sunny day than a picnic? The great thing about picnics is that you can have one almost anywhere – in the park, in the woods, or even in your yard. Food always tastes better outdoors. The only rule should be that everyone has to help prepare the food.

Check the weather forecast the day before you plan on having a picnic. If the forecast is cold or rainy, why not have an indoor picnic instead?

Don't despair if you don't have a traditional picnic basket on hand, but do make sure you have other suitable storage for your food and drinks. Coolers are excellent for keeping food and drinks chilled.

Take something to sit on. Unless you're heading to a picnic spot with chairs and tables provided, you'll need a blanket or sheet for your food and to sit down on. Take a few cushions for extra comfort.

When picking a picnic spot, always make sure you are allowed to picnic there.

Take a plastic bag with you to put any trash in, and take it with you when you leave. Always clean up after you have finished and leave the picnic spot just as you found it.

Tip from Mom: Make your picnic even more fun by giving it a theme. Invite lots of friends and have a competition to see who brings the most popular dish.

Outdoor games are a great way to liven up a picnic. Try Giddy Running (see pages 107 to 108) or a game of Wildlife Bingo (see pages 92 to 93).

Here is a recipe for picnic pastries that are easy to eat outdoors.

MOUTHWATERING PICNIC TURNOVERS

These cheese turnovers are great for a picnic, as they taste really delicious when eaten cold. They are also yummy when still warm from the oven.

You will need:

For the dough:

- 2 cups plain flour • 1/2 teaspoon salt
  - 1/2 cup butter or margarine
- 2 to 3 tablespoons cold water • 1 beaten egg

For the filling:

- 1 cup boiled new potatoes, cut into cubes
  - 1 cup cheddar cheese, cut into cubes
    - 1 leek, boiled and sliced

 Preheat the oven to 400°F.

First, mix the flour and salt in a bowl. Then cut the margarine or butter into small pieces and rub it into the flour until the mixture resembles crumbs. Add the water, a little bit at a time, and knead until the mixture forms a soft pastry dough.

Cover the bowl with plastic wrap and place in the fridge for an hour.

Meanwhile, make the filling by mixing the cheese, potatoes, and leeks in a bowl.

After an hour, roll out the dough on a clean, floured surface. Cut out circles, using a side plate (about 6 inches in diameter) as a template. Alternatively, divide the dough into four parts and roll each piece into a circle of the same diameter.

Put a spoonful of filling in the middle of each circle. Fold the edges of the circle together over the top of the filling, crimping them together with your fingers to form an enclosed turnover shape.

Place your turnovers on a baking sheet and brush them with the egg. Bake them in the oven for 20 minutes, or until golden brown.

Let the turnovers cool before placing them in an airtight container all ready for your picnic. Alternatively, enjoy them while they are still warm as you picnic on your carpet!

Warning: The filling inside these turnovers stays hot for longer than you think, so make sure you test the center before taking a bite.

Play Wildlife Bingo

Turn an everyday walk in the park into a nail-biting adventure by playing Wildlife Bingo.

Before leaving the house, find a sheet of paper for each person playing the game and divide it into a grid of 9, 12, or 16 squares.

In each square of the grid, draw or write the name of an animal or plant that you might spot on the walk. For example, if you are walking in the woods you could include types of birds, flowers, mammals, and trees that you are likely to see.

Make each sheet different so that not all the animals and plants are the same. If players are of different ages, you should think about putting the easier things to find on the younger ones' sheets. For older or more experienced players, you can be more specific as to the wildlife they have to spot, such as a certain species of wildflower or mushroom.

Give each player a pen and a grid and, as you walk along, mark off each item as you see it.

Make sure all the players know when the game has begun, so that they don't start marking their cards early. There must be a witness to each sighting whenever possible. Continue on the walk very quietly and carefully, making sure you don't miss or scare off any possible sightings.

The first player to cross off everything on his or her grid wins the game and says, "Bingo!" Be careful not to shout though, as you don't want to scare off any of the animals for the next game.

Make sure your bingo grids are seasonal and in keeping with your environment. There is no point in spending the day hunting for an autumn leaf in the spring or looking for a bear at the beach.

Paint Your China

Spruce up old plates or mugs with your own stylish designs. If you don't have any spare plates or mugs around the house, visit your local secondhand store. There are sure to be some plates and cups in need of a makeover.

You will need:

• paper • colored pencils or felt-tip markers
• a plain plate, mug, or bowl • brushes • some sheets of newspaper • ceramic paints (found online or in craft stores)

Tip from Mom: If you are planning to use your redecorated item for food or drinks, make sure the ceramic paint you use is safe for contact with food.

Look in some art or antiques books to get inspiration. You could make a striking, colorful design like Picasso or a more refined blue-willow pattern. Alternatively, you could make personalized mugs for your friends and family.

Test out a few designs on paper, using colored pencils or markers first. This way you can decide the effect you want before you start to paint.

Wash and dry your plate thoroughly to remove any greasy fingerprints or residue that could keep the paint from sticking to the surface.

Lay out your paints, brushes, and the item to be painted on a surface protected with newspaper or a mat. Sketch out your design onto the plate using a pencil first and then begin to paint.

When you have finished painting, leave your masterpiece to dry overnight to make sure your design has completely set.

Before you can use your plate, most ceramic paints need to be baked in the oven. For this, follow the manufacturer's instructions given on the side of the paint containers. Make sure you let your work of art cool after baking and wash again before use.

Tip from Mom: Why stop at plates? You could do flowerpots, egg cups, or vases. Many ceramic paints can also be used on glass, so why not personalize your own drinking glass or make one for a friend?

Seriously Super Smoothies

Store-bought smoothies are usually expensive, but this quick, simple drink is inexpensive to make at home, and it's full of fresh, natural ingredients and packed with vitamins.

You will need:

- 1 ripe banana • a knife
- 1 small container of plain or fruit yogurt
- 1 glass of milk
- a handful of soft fruit (strawberries, raspberries, and blackberries work well)

Slice the banana and put in a blender. Add the yogurt and fruit and blend for a minute. Add the milk and blend for a few seconds more. Pour and enjoy!

Make a Prickly Hedgehog

This pin-covered pet is a practical pal in anyone's sewing box. Either keep him all to yourself, or give him to a friend or relative. He may look cute, but don't give him a hug or you could get pricked.

You will need:

• tracing paper • a pencil • scissors • black and brown felt
• chalk • needle and black thread
• old tights or more fabric scraps for stuffing
• 2 buttons or googly eyes from a craft store

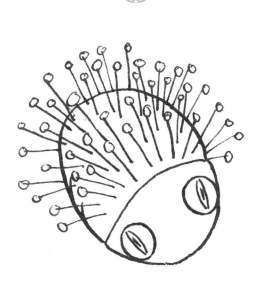

First you need to make the pattern for your prickly friend. Place the tracing paper over the pattern below and draw around it using a pencil. Trace around each shape separately so that you end up with three shapes on your paper. Cut these out carefully using scissors.

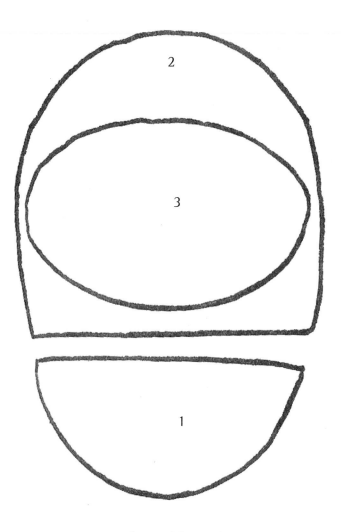

Place shape 1 on a piece of black felt and draw around it with chalk. Repeat this on the brown felt with shapes 2 and 3, and then cut out your shapes.

Using a running stitch (see page 14), sew felt shape 1 to felt shape 2 along the straight edge as shown. Secure your stitches at the beginning and end of sewing with a few stitches on top of each other.

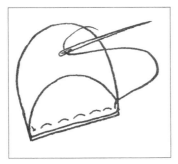

Sew the black and brown top piece to felt shape 3 with the seam facing in so that it will be inside your pincushion.

Gather the edges of the top piece as you sew to make them fit together. Stop before you have sewn all the way around, leaving a hole to insert the stuffing.

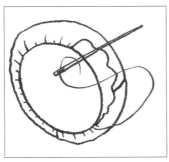

Fill your cushion with stuffing until it is firm and then sew up the hole.

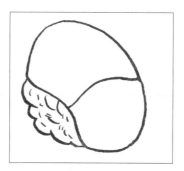

Sew on the buttons for your hedgehog's eyes.

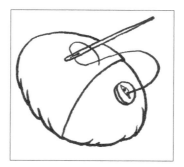

All that's missing now are his quills, so fill the hedgehog with all of your pins.

Make the Perfect Omelette

Omelettes are the original fast food and can provide a filling, nutritious meal in minutes. Simple as they seem, it's easy to make them too heavy or too thin.

You will need:

- salt and pepper • 3 eggs
- a pinch of mixed herbs
- a pat of butter
- an 8-inch frying pan (a 6-inch pan for a two-egg omelette)
- a fork • a spatula

Break the eggs into a bowl, add the salt, pepper, and herbs, and then beat the egg mixture lightly with a fork.

 Place the pan over medium heat. Add the butter and then tilt the pan over the heat so that the melting butter coats the bottom.

Turn up the heat and pour in the beaten eggs.

Allow the mixture to set a little and then use a spatula to push it away from the sides. Tip the pan so that any uncooked egg on top runs to the edges. When the top is almost cooked, take the spatula and fold the omelette in half. Tip it onto a warm plate and serve immediately.

Tip from Mom: Once you have mastered the perfect omelette, experiment with different fillings. Any of the following ingredients can be added to the egg mixture:

- chopped ham • chopped cooked bacon
- grated cheese (approximately 1 ounce per egg)
- chopped tomatoes • potatoes, precooked and chopped

Tip from Mom: The key to a light, fluffy omelette is to make sure the butter is hot before you add the eggs. You should also always use the right-size pan.

Grow an Avocado Plant

Avocados make beautiful indoor plants and will grow from the pit of the fruit you eat.

You will need:

- a few ripe avocados • a knife
- some jars or a wide-necked bottle
- water • toothpicks • a 6-inch plant pot
- potting soil • sand

Tip from Mom: Not all avocado pits will grow into successful plants, so it pays to have a few spares.

Cut open an avocado by piercing the skin and then running the knife around the pit, being careful not to damage it. Open gently and remove the pit. Scoop out the flesh and enjoy later, or make "Avocado Ghouls" (see pages 40 to 41).

Wash the pit and insert three toothpicks into its side. The toothpicks should be evenly spaced and about halfway down from the wider end.

Using the toothpicks as a rest, suspend the pit, pointed end up, in a jar filled with water. Place the jar on a warm windowsill. Keep the jar filled to the brim with water at all times, so that half of the pit is underwater.

In two or three weeks, the pit should crack. In another four weeks, a root will grow from the submerged end. Shortly afterward, a stem will begin to grow.

When the root is at least 2 inches long and the stem is at least 4 inches tall, plant the pit in a pot measuring 6 inches or more in diameter. Good potting soil should be used. Mix three parts of soil with one part of sand. The pot should be kept wet for the first week. After that the soil should be watered once a week and kept moist.

Avocado plants can grow into small bushes or taller trees. If you want a bush, pinch off the tip of the plant and the tips of new branches, and more branches will grow. If you would prefer a small tree, just let it grow upward.

Don't wait around for your plant to bear fruit, though. It could take years, or it may never happen at all.

Knot a Lanyard Key Ring

Get knotting and make a really cool key ring — all it takes is a little practice.

You'll need:

* 2 different-colored plastic lanyard strings
* a split ring that takes keys
* a medium-size bead (match it with your lanyard colors if you can)

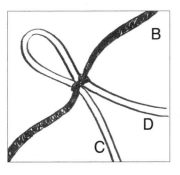

Step 1. Make a small loop in the middle of one string and then tie the different-colored string around the loop in a knot. This will be the loop you attach the split ring to.

Step 2. You now have four lanyard strings, A and B in one color, C and D in a second color. Arrange the colors so that they are opposite each other in a cross.

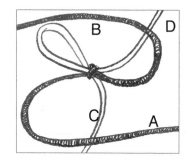

Step 3. Make a loop in string A and a loop in string B as shown. Now thread string C through loop A and string D through loop B and pull tight. The knot should now look like a checkered square.

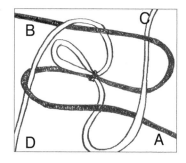

Step 4. Repeat step three, but this time make loops with C and D and then thread A and B through the loops you have made and tighten.

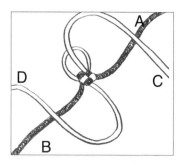

Continue your lanyard, alternating the knots made in steps 3 and 4 until it is as long as you want. Leave a 2 1/2 inch length at the end of each string. To add a bead, thread your bead over all four strings before making a final knot.

Play Giddy Running

The only thing more fun than getting as dizzy as you can and then trying to walk in a straight line is watching someone else do it. A good game for the backyard, make sure you have lots of soft cushions so that you don't land with too much of a bump.

You will need:

- a large, flat grassy space in a backyard or park
- lots of pillows and soft things to land on
- a broomstick

Lay the cushions out in two straight lines about 3 feet apart. This will mark the course.

Stand at the beginning of the course and hold the broomstick to your chest vertically, so that the end of it comes about 12 inches above your head. Look up at the end of the broom and spin around as fast as you can five times. The other players should count out loud as you spin.

Stop when you are facing the beginning of the course and drop the broom carefully to the side. Now try to walk (or run) as fast as you can in a straight line to the end of the course. This is not as easy as you think, as you will be very dizzy and will probably stumble as soon as you start.

The goal of giddy running is to get as far along the course as possible without touching the pillows on the sides. If you reach the end, see if you can run back.

Make Fortune Cookies

Fortune cookies are delicious cookies with a surprise inside. They are great at parties and can be even more fun if you write your own fortunes to put in them.

You will need:

- 2 egg whites • 1/2 teaspoon vanilla extract
- 1 pinch salt • 2 1/2 tablespoons flour
- 1/4 cup sugar • a sheet of plain paper • scissors
- a pen or pencil

THE FORTUNES

Before you start to cook, cut the paper into strips of around 3 inches by 1/4 inch so they are slim enough to fit inside the cookies.

Write your fortunes. Make them as general as possible, as you don't know who will pick each cookie. Never put bad fortunes in, as they might be taken seriously.

Traditional messages include, "You will live long and prosper," or "Seven will be your lucky number this week."

THE COOKIES

 Preheat the oven to 400°F.

Put the egg whites in a large bowl with the vanilla extract. Whisk until fluffy but not stiff. Add the flour, salt, and sugar, then mix together.

Place teaspoonfuls of the batter 4 inches apart on a baking sheet and tilt so that they make circles of about 3 inches in diameter.

 Bake for 5 minutes in the oven or until the cookies are golden at the edges. In the meantime, prepare the next sheet and put these in the oven when the first batch is ready.

 Take the cookies out of the oven and quickly remove them with a wide spatula, placing them upside down on a wooden board. Put the fortune onto the cookie, close to the middle, and fold the cookie in half.

Holding the folded cookie in both hands, between your thumb and index fingers, fold in half again so that it is in quarters. If your cookie is a little stiff, pull the ends down over the rim of a glass or the handle of a wooden spoon, until the ends meet. The opened side of the fortune cookie should be facing up toward you.

Always use cold baking sheets, as warm ones will make the cookies bake too quickly.

You must work quickly with the cookies in the final stages as they set very quickly. For best results make three or four cookies at a time.

Tip from Mom: If you can, wear a pair of cotton gloves to help you handle the cookies when they are hot.

Make Your Own Craft Kit

There's no need to buy an expensive kit from a craft store when you can make your own. Start by designing the box you want to keep your kit in. Cover a shoe box in wrapping paper or decoupage (see pages 124 to 126). Or cover it with fabric as described below for a stunning transformation.

FABRIC-COVERED BOX

You will need:

- 1 shoe box with lid • a ruler • paper • a pencil
- scissors • 3 feet of fabric
- spray adhesive or strong craft glue
- a sheet of upholstery foam for lid (optional)

Measure around all four sides of the box, then add an inch to the total length. Measure the depth and, again, add an inch.

Using these measurements, draw a long rectangle on a sheet of paper and cut it out. Then pin your template to the fabric and cut around it.

Place the bottom of the box on the fabric and draw around it. Cut out this rectangle and put it aside (you will use this to cover the bottom of the box once the sides have been covered).

Spray or paint a thin layer of glue onto one of the long sides of the box and smooth on the longer rectangle of fabric. Make sure you leave a little fabric at the top and bottom to turn over at the end to make neat edges.

Now move around the box, applying glue to each side and carefully smoothing on the fabric. Try not to leave any creases or air bubbles under the material.

When you reach the end, fold the remainder of the material under itself and glue down, so that the fabric joins neatly at the corner.

At the top corners, cut narrow triangles in the overlapping fabric and stick down to the inside of the box.

Turn the box over, spray or spread glue over the bottom of the box, and smooth on the smaller rectangle of fabric.

Place the lid of your box on your fabric and draw around this. Measure the depth of the lid and add this to the edge of each of the lid's sides plus an extra inch to tuck under. If you would like a padded lid, glue the foam to the lid of the box first.

Cut the fabric into a rectangle for the lid and then apply glue to the top of the lid or padding and stick on your fabric.

Glue the fabric to the long sides and then fold down at the corners and glue on to the short sides. Finish by cutting small triangles in the corners of overlapping material and gluing the fabric down inside.

ITEMS FOR YOUR KIT

Now that you have a beautiful box to keep your collage and design materials in, here are a few suggestions for the contents:

- fabric scraps • ribbons • paper • pens • buttons
- beads • straws • string • Popsicle sticks
- glitter • glitter glue • wrapping paper
- silver foil • wallpaper
- magazine cuttings • gift bows

Keep containers with lids, such as those that poster paints come in, for storing beads, buttons, and other items. If anyone you know has a nondigital camera, ask them for the empty film cases, and keep the little tubes that you buy glitter and craft materials in for reuse.

Disguise the Spy

Make your own undercover agent and dress him for top secret missions.

You will need:

- a photocopier or tracing paper and a pencil
- cardboard • glue • scissors
- clear contact paper • felt-tip markers

Photocopy pages 116 and 117, enlarging them if you wish. If you do not have access to a photocopier, trace around the items using tracing paper and a pencil.

Glue the spy to a piece of cardboard, color him in, and cover with clear contact paper. Cut him out carefully and fold along the dotted line to make him able to stand.

To make his basic spy clothes, color and cut out his hat, coat, and pants. Fit them to his body using the tabs.

Your spy is now ready to begin his investigations, however, he will need more clothes in order to remain undercover. Decide on his mission: He could need to locate an enemy agent at a dance club or even head off into space.

Draw your designs on paper and color them before cutting them out. Include short tabs on each garment that can fold over the spy's body.

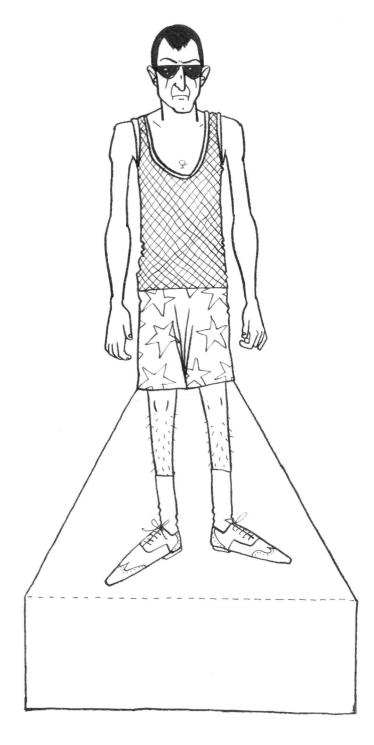

Banana Nut Bread

Banana nut bread is a family favorite and perfect for any picnic.

You will need:

- 3 large, soft bananas • 2 cups flour
- 2 teaspoons baking powder
- 1/2 cup butter • 1/2 cup superfine sugar
- 1/2 teaspoon salt • 2 eggs
- 1 cup chopped walnuts
- a loaf pan (9 inches by 5 inches), lightly greased with butter

Preheat the oven to 350°F.

 While the oven is warming up, peel the bananas and mash them with a fork in a large bowl.

Add the rest of the ingredients, except for the nuts. Mix until thoroughly blended, then add the nuts and mix again.

Pour the mixture into your loaf pan and bake in the oven for 55 minutes.

You can tell if the loaf is done by inserting a toothpick into the middle of it. If it comes out clean, your banana nut bread is done.

Cool on a wire rack.

Make Your Very Own Teddy Bear

Why buy a cuddly toy from a store when you can create a cute companion unlike any other? Here's how to make a lovable plush friend.

You will need:

- a photocopier or tracing paper and a pencil
- 2 pieces of cardboard • scissors • glue
- 14 inches by 14 inches furry fabric and matching thread
- a felt-tip marker • some pins
- a needle • stuffing or old tights
- eyes and nose (found in craft stores), or black buttons

TEDDY TEMPLATES

Start by photocopying the front and back pattern from pages 122 and 123. If you do not have access to a photocopier, trace the patterns. Glue the patterns on to cardboard and leave to dry. When the glue is dry, cut around the outline of the pattern to make your teddy templates.

Place the front template on the back of the furry fabric and draw around it with the marker. When you have drawn around one side, turn the template over and draw around it the other way. This will give your bear a right and a left side. Repeat this with the template for the back of the bear.

Cut out your pieces. You should end up with four pieces — two front and two back.

IT'S SEW TIME

With the furry sides of the fabric facing each other, pin the front pieces of the bear together. Sew the two pieces together down the middle from point A to point B, using the backstitch (see page 15), leaving a seam of 1/4 inch around the edge. Do the same with the back section, sewing this time from point C to D, leaving an opening in the back seam, as shown on the pattern.

If using a nose and eyes from a craft shop, attach them to the front of the bear, following the instructions on the pack.

Pin the back section to the front, furry sides together, and sew around the outsides. When you have finished, turn the unstuffed bear furry side out.

GET STUFFED

Now fill your teddy by pushing the stuffing into the hole you left in his back. Use lots of stuffing for a firmer bear and less for a softer one. Use a pencil to poke the stuffing into any awkward nooks and crannies like the arms and legs. Sew up the hole in the back.

Sew on two buttons for eyes if your bear doesn't have them already.

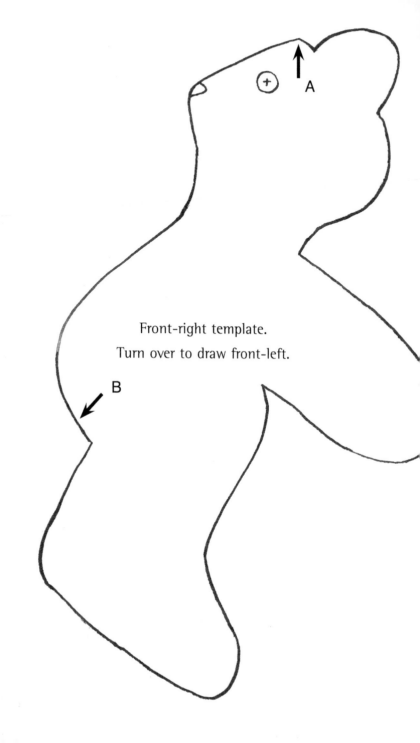

Front-right template.
Turn over to draw front-left.

A

B

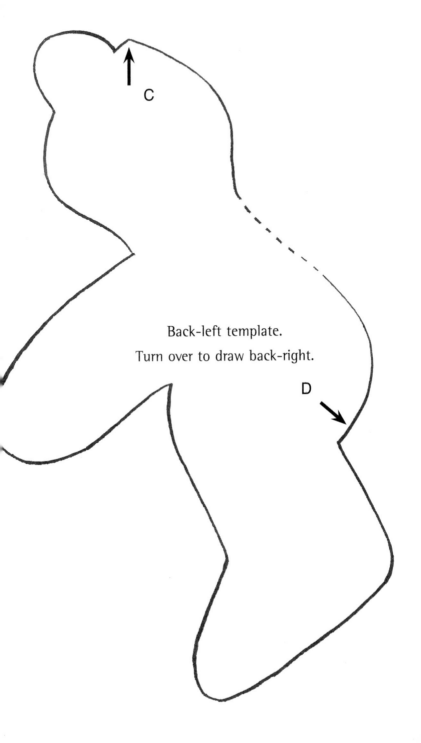

C

Back-left template.
Turn over to draw back-right.

D

Funk Up Your Furniture

Breathe new life into a tired piece of furniture with this beautiful craft that dates back to the twelfth century.

The name *decoupage* comes from the French word *découper*, which means to cut out. By cutting out, then pasting pictures on a wardrobe, chair, or chest of drawers, you can give your furniture a stunning finish.

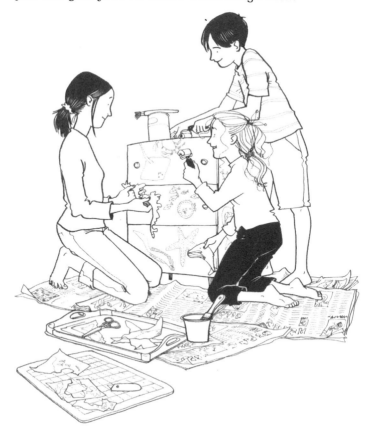

You will need:

• paper and a pencil • thick cardboard or a cutting board
• a craft knife or scissors
• an item of furniture (chest of drawers, chair, table, or
nightstand)
• sandpaper • dustcloth
• emulsion paint in a color that complements the
pictures (for example, a shade of green if you are
using floral or leaf designs)
• pictures for your design (wrapping paper, wallpaper,
posters, or magazine pictures) • a small paintbrush
• decoupage glue (a special glue found in any craft store)
• a small roller from a hardware or craft store • water

Let your imagination run wild for a few minutes as
you plan your decoupage design. Sketch out a few
possible patterns on a piece of paper before picking
your favorite. Your pictures can stand alone or overlap
if you wish.

Before you start, make sure you put thick cardboard
or a cutting board underneath the pictures to
protect the surface below. Cut around the outlines of the
images with the craft knife or scissors.

Wear a mask to prevent dust inhalation. Then sand down
your furniture, removing any dust with a damp cloth. In a
well-ventilated area, apply a thin coat of emulsion paint to
the furniture and wait for it to dry.

Arrange your cutout pictures on a table to make up your chosen design. Take the paintbrush and coat the back of each image with your decoupage glue. Then paint a thin layer of glue on the area you wish to stick the pictures.

Place the pictures on the furniture, using your fingers to gently smooth down the paper and push out any wrinkles. Run the roller over the cutouts to ensure any bubbles or wrinkles disappear.

Continue adding new pictures and smoothing them out until they are all in place. Now leave the pictures to dry.

When you are certain everything is thoroughly dry, coat the whole piece of furniture with your decoupage glue, diluted by one part of water to three parts glue, or according to the glue's instructions.

Add more diluted decoupage glue or a clear varnish until the edges of the pictures are smooth. Allow the coating to dry.

Find the perfect spot for your newly revamped furniture. Make sure its eye-catching decoration can be seen from as many angles as possible!

Tip from Mom: Why not pick a bargain piece of furniture from a garage sale, then use decoupage to turn it into a treasured family possession?

Meet Mr. Turf Top

Give an old pair of Mom's stockings a terrific turf toupee with this fun gardening project that'll keep everyone amused for weeks on end.

You will need:

- old nylon stockings • a pair of scissors
- grass seed • sawdust • rubber bands
- eyes made from cardboard or googly eyes
(available in craft stores)
- lips cut from felt or fabric
- a bowl of water • a small saucer

For each Mr. Turf Top: Cut off one leg of the stockings and discard the rest. Pour a large spoonful of grass seed into the foot and spread it around the toe area. Stuff the end of the stocking with sawdust until the "head" is the size you want.

Secure the bottom with a rubber band, or simply tie it in a knot. Make sure that the seed is spread evenly where you want the hair to grow. Then create a nose by pinching a small section of nylon and sawdust and wrapping a rubber band around it. Glue on eyes and lips.

Lastly, soak Mr. Turf Top in a small bowl of water so that the sawdust is damp, then sit him comfortably in the saucer and watch his hair grow.

Don't forget to add water to the saucer every so often and give Mr. Turf Top an occasional trim.

Fresh Pasta Feast

This recipe makes delicious fresh fettuccine for four people, and it's perfect to serve up with Mama's Meatballs (see page 130).

You will need:

• 2 cups flour • 2 eggs • a pinch of salt

Combine the flour and salt in a large bowl. Crack the eggs into another bowl and beat lightly with a fork. Make a well in the middle of the flour, then pour in the beaten eggs. Stir together until firm. At this stage, if your dough feels dry, add a little water. If it seems sticky, add some extra flour.

Place the dough onto a floured surface and knead thoroughly for 10 minutes until smooth and shiny. Cover in plastic wrap and leave to rest for 15 minutes.

Unwrap the dough and roll it out on a floured surface into a long rectangle shape that is very thin. Dust the pasta sheet with flour to prevent sticking and carefully fold the narrow edge of the sheet over by 1 1/2 inches. Continue folding until the whole sheet is rolled up into a long tube.

Take a knife and cut strips of pasta 1/2 inch wide from the folded piece until you reach the end. Unfold the strips and leave to dry for a few minutes before cooking.

Cook the pasta in boiling water for 4 to 5 minutes, tasting a piece to see if it is ready. Drain and serve.

Mama's Meatballs

This has long been a staple dish in parts of southern Italy and has become a family favorite in the United States, too.

You will need:

- 2 slices of white bread
- 1 tablespoon chopped fresh parsley
- 1/2 cup grated Parmesan cheese
- 1 pound lean ground beef • salt and pepper • 2 eggs
- 1 tablespoon olive oil • 1 onion, finely chopped
- 2 14-ounce cans chopped tomatoes • 1 pound spaghetti

This recipe will feed four to five hungry people.

Using a food processor, grind the bread into fine crumbs. Add the parsley and half of the Parmesan cheese and stir together. Add the beef and some freshly milled black pepper.

Break the eggs into the bowl and beat. Add the egg to the meat and blend the mixture together with your hands.

Roll the mixture into balls the size of a large walnut and place on a baking sheet covered in plastic wrap. Put to one side.

Heat the olive oil in a large saucepan and fry the onion until soft. Add the tomatoes and some salt and pepper. Bring to a boil and turn down the heat to simmer for ten minutes. Drop in the meatballs one by one and then cover the pan. Simmer for 1 hour.

After about 40 minutes, cook the spaghetti according to the instructions on the package or cook your fresh fettuccine (see page 129). Drain the pasta and place in a serving dish. Stir in the cooked meatballs and remaining cheese. Serve immediately.

Tip from Mom: If you prefer a sweeter sauce, add half a teaspoon of sugar to your sauce before you add the meatballs.

Haircare at Home

AVOCADO HAIR TREATMENT

Avocados are packed with vitamins and can give your hair a real treat, rehydrating it and leaving it smooth and shiny.

You will need:

- 1 small jar of mayonnaise (not the low-fat type!)
- 1/2 a ripe avocado • a shower cap or plastic wrap

Put the ingredients in a bowl and, using your hands or a spoon, squash the avocado into the mayonnaise until it forms a green paste.

Smooth over your hair, from the roots to the tips. Put on a shower cap or wrap your hair in plastic wrap.

For hair in need of extra-deep conditioning, wrap a hot, damp towel over the cap or plastic wrap. This may require two pairs of hands.

Wait for 20 minutes before rinsing with lots of clean, warm water.

LAVENDER HAIR RINSE

This not only smells great, but lavender is thought to be a natural remedy for dandruff. Pour 1/2 cup of dried lavender into a pan with 2 cups of water. Bring to a boil and simmer for 3 minutes, then allow the mixture to cool. Use the lavender water as a hair rinse after washing your hair and leave it on for 15 minutes before rinsing with water.

ROSEMARY HAIR RINSE

Boil a large saucepan of water, then take a bunch of fresh rosemary and add it to the pan. Simmer for half an hour and leave to cool before straining.

This should only be used on dark hair, as it can darken blond hair. It adds shine, helps soothe itchy scalps, and smells really great.

The "Would You Rather?" Game

This is a great game that can be played anywhere and that should spark some very interesting and bizarre conversations.

Each player takes turns presenting the other players with an imaginary scenario. The scenario has two possible outcomes, which players have to choose between. The answers "neither" or "both" are not allowed.

The scenarios can be as crazy and unrealistic as you like. In fact, the quirkier they are, the better.

For example:

- Would you rather have a tiger or a crocodile as a pet?

- Would you rather your left arm be made out of Jell-O or out of cake?

- Would you rather sit in a bath filled with maggots or eat worms?

This game works best if you make your options really difficult to choose between. They could be really yucky, really yummy, really scary, or really funny. This is a fantastic way to find out more about one another, and there are no winners or losers. So what are you waiting for? Get those brain-boggling questions ready!

Be sure to look for:

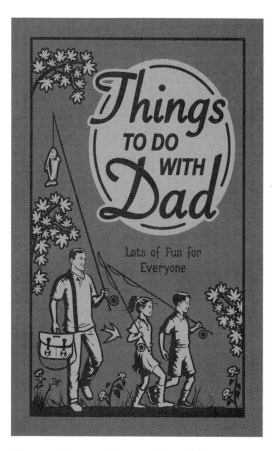

There will never be another dull moment
when Dad's around!